HOUSEHOLDER

HOUSEHOLDER

Gerard Woodward

Chatto & Windus
LONDON

Lines Review
D.

Published in 1991 by
Chatto & Windus Ltd
20 Vauxhall Bridge Road
London SW1V 2SA

A CIP catalogue record for this book is available
from the British Library

ISBN 0 7011 3758 4

Some of these poems have appeared in *Argo*, *Encounter*,
Orbis, *Poetry Nottingham*, *Poetry Review*, *Rialto*, the
Spectator, *Stand*, *The Times Literary Supplement* and *Verse*; in the
pamphlet *The Unwriter* (Sycamore Press, 1989); and in *New
Voices* (Anvil 1990)

Photoset by
Cambridge Composing (UK) Ltd
Cambridge

Printed in Great Britain
by Mackays of Chatham PLC,
Chatham, Kent.

9547
(23.04.91)
C

Contents

HOUSEHOLDER

For Suzanne

I WINDOW-BREAKER

ROUGH SEA

We are the dangerous holidaymakers,
The violent tourists
Who come to these resorts only in bad weather,

When the sea is a vista of troublesome babies
Resisting their cradles and staying awake,
Pests who chuck small bombs

And give us their saline rain.
We shun umbrellas,
Scorn scarves and hoods,

But hang on to shilling telescopes
For dear life when the big waves come,
The sea's fists thrust up in triumph.

We gather in crowds
At the pier's head and watch
The conflicts erupt,

And laugh as the English Channel
Spits in our faces and the prom
Is overrun by frothy hoodlums,

Gutters alive with sprats and mackerel,
Civic fountains wondering what they're for,
Crabs dashing from the paths of taxis,

Winkles and mussels instead of hailstones.
We are the destructive holidaymakers
Who like to watch the sea breaking up

Before our eyes (and who will mend it?)
We like to see the naval war memorials
Under threat, the sea's artillery

At full stretch, ordinary people
Ordained as monks beneath their jackets.
We are the tough tourists

Who like the indecent assault of easterly gales,
Who detest tans and smiling weathermen,
Who love the smack in the face and cut lip of a rough sea.

A PROSPECT OF DOGS

Remark, the dog walks
Under threat of death
By hanging.

And the doberman called Clausewitz
Thrills the children
With his cemetery of teeth,

While the graveyard mastiff
Sniffs the rootless flowers
And pisses them to death.

Watch their abrupt wars
Among daisies and cricket pitches,
Or, naked in the negotiating chamber,

How they conduct the diplomacy
Of smells. Shy of meeting
Eye to eye, like profiles

Vying with candlestick,
They are interested in the dead
Pieces of each other.

Running fool's errands
They forbid you
To rid yourself of anything.

MEVAGISSEY BAKERY

The doughnut with its red heart
Has come alive like the fish skeletons
Whose guts are rebuilt of mud.

Jamheart, mudheart, reflect each other
As the bakery window reflects the sea
Like a huge transparent postcard

And sees the town's stone mouth
Drink a mixture of tide and boats
Who spear themselves in the mud.

And childhood evolves here for each
Boat is a cupboard of toys,
Balloons, footballs, flags, windmills

Attaching themselves to wooden castles.
In this mud playground
Crabs are knitting

Like the men up on the walls
Where the quay becomes a haberdashery of linens
As though the stone had spawned seed to drift

Like old man's beard.
And the fine nets pull the sea into the town
Where the salt pulse transforms each shop

Into an imitation of itself,
The butcher's with its sawdust floor
Is a tiny beach bathed in blood

And the bakery whose yeast rises like the tide
Evolves cakes in spirals like sea snails,
Decorates its fancies with tiny sugar seahorses.

The bakery throbs with jam and yeast,
It is the town's warm heart
And feeds the journey from childhood to death

From harbour to graveyard
Where each death is marked by a fish bone;
Where, in their mud voyage

In wooden submarines, human bones
Are rebuilt of mud and through their
White periscopes sniff a mixture of salt and yeast.

WINDOW-BREAKER

Causing a riot of liberation,
Causing his own Kristallnacht,
Though he broke the Arabian Scent Shop
As well as the kosher butchers,
He unlocked the windows with his bricks.
'Let the smell of the shops
Be on the streets!' he yelled,
The jailer, rattling his bricks.
The windows bloomed with complex flowers
And dropped their sharp seeds in cones
Like sultans weighing themselves.
He just wanted the streets
To reek of shop smell.
He rang the windows like gongs
And smells of hide, paper,
Blood, linen, cakes and moonstone
Fumbled out and raced with him
Along the glittering streets, glittering
Like a diamond cutter's work surface.
The constable, in his shining buttons,
Was amazed, a few minutes later,
To find the window of the jewellers gone
But all the gems still sleeping
On their pillows.

MATRIARCH

The first astronomer's wife
Asked him to turn

His attention to her. And so
He slid his telescope

Into her cunt and watched.
The stars there were red,

Spiral galaxies of blood trembled
In her hot, dark heavens.

He surmised he saw the future
When a city came, full

Of singing babies building
Their city bigger and bigger.

And then from the first
Astronomer's wife's vulva fanned

A kinship diagram, a web
Of triangles and circles that spread

So wide it seemed as if the world
Was pulling on a fishnet stocking.

She shook, winded by the thought
Of her gut full of impending cities,

'Sew it up!' she cried, 'sew up
The gap!' And he obliged

Because he shook too.
It hurt. She bit her lip.

She bit her tears
But that stitched seam

Was a door slammed
On the future. A long line

Of silence formed as a huge
Genealogical pyramid vanished

Into air. Cities had holes
In them, as if got at

By moths. Postal districts
Disappeared, London lost some N's

And E's. The first astronomer
And his wife sighed, no longer

Appalled by the thought of the baby
Inside the baby inside the baby,

That blubbery, pink continuum.
Her states and wars died with her.

But it makes no difference to us.
We're here anyway, and the gaps were soon

Filled by wives incontinent with
Nations, flatulent with cities

Pouring out of them. They didn't see.
They didn't watch. They hadn't telescopes.

THE BRONTE BROTHER

I hear them at night whispering
In their odorous and dark sisterhood,
'How will we get away?' Amid the comfort

Of their shared bed, the moonlight
Making beautiful African hills of the bedclothes.
Their hair seems sewn to their heads,

The beautiful stitching that divides their hair
With such a straight white line,
Their scalps are so pale.

When I see the crowns of their heads on the pillow
It is three faint white lines each at an angle
To the other like half-formed lettering.

And one fears she will be the last to die,
And one uses her clothes
As a feathery shadow. (I lie

In the moonlight in the garden
And I play with the light to see
If I can feel it with my eyes shut

Moving my hand smoothly from shadow to light
And when I feel the moon's heat I open my eyes
And see this exquisite blue candelabra

Hanging in the dark garden air.)
And I imagine them in jewels and metal necklaces
As though an oval mirror had been

Broken over them and they wore its fragments
As acts of heroism.
And I will be drunk on moonlight

As I watch their safe sleep
And the strong smell of their young hair
And their paper-white scalps.

My breath passes in clouds over them.
One day I will do a picture of them,
Without their hands, of course,

And I will fold my painting over
So that the future will make
A ghost cross, a faint cross

Across the face of the painting,
A flaking cross of missing paint
Like the beautiful seams of their heads

That the future will unfold my sisters
As they watch moonlight through a window frame
And see them as bearers of an invisible cross.

HAMLET ON PIGGYBACK

He clung to my back
Like old age. Whispered
Faster, faster, faster.

Other times, he insisted
On kissing me full
On the lips like a

Miniature wife. Asked
What it is like to grow
Old, old, old

(All of seven years of age),
I told him princes
Don't grow old, only kings

And he seemed pleased
With this. I charged
Through leaves, his stallion,

And we made
Pictures out of clouds,
Weasel, camel, whale,

God knows but the talk
Always got back to the ground
And its contents.

Forty thousand brothers
Would have found him
Dreary, his only friend

A fool with faces
On sticks. I always felt
He would go to bed

At noon. The very day
He was born our new
Gravemaker came.

THE UNWRITER

In sleep she unwrites letters
Clearing pages of their words
With a pen that sucks up ink.

These letters fall to her bed
From sacks sewn by murderers
Making her eiderdown

The whole world's sorting office.
Letters from Italy, The Lizard,
Golders Green and Irkutsk,

From dentists wanting new clothes,
From sculptors who've run out of nails,
From mothers wondering about

The faces of their sons,
Letters *par avion*,
Sea mail that takes months

In its long swim.
Stamps show kings
And birds, great architects

And wild flowers
Franked with symbols
Of memory and speed.

Letters need no words,
It is the posting that has meaning,
The journey and the opening of envelopes.

She relieves these of their
Burdens of addresses,
Smooths out pens' indentations.

They are delivered to all houses
By old men who stoop
Like the Santa Claus of the door,

The blizzard on their backs
Making the whole world
Snow blind.

While her great store
Of unstuck ink
Floods her dark cellar

Like coal made liquid.
When she has finished dreaming
She dives into this.

THE ENORMOUS GARDEN

The gardeners have lost
Their borders. The absence
Of fences after last

Night's storms has blurred
All gardens together
And now the poor things

Are pruning wrong roses,
Wondering how flowers
Can change colour so quickly.

They are weeding
Out strange beds,
Using next-door's lumbago

Shears and secateurs,
Crashing their mowers together.
Who could have foreseen it,

This enormous garden
Where greenhouses cannot
Keep secrets, strawberries

Are no longer coveted?
Not even the compilers
Of seed catalogues

Predicted this. And now
The gardeners are starting
To love it, are saving

Their snails from eating
Dangerous dinners, planning
Lawns that span the Earth

And flower-beds big
As cities. Except,
That is, for one

By the compost. He hammers
A stake into the ground
Cursing with a mouthful of nails.

THE FLOWER MURDERS

He pushed her face into the rose
Saying, 'God is love'.

Scotland Yard knew them
As the Flower Murders

Because every strangled girl
Held a little nosegay

Like British Rail bridesmaids.
The killer, they thought, must be

A henpecked husband nagged
Into forever buying bouquets.

But he was not.
He was the curator at Kew,

Who knew how hard it is
To love the flower

Without killing, that is, picking it.
Murder is an act of love.

As a young botanist in the archipelagos
He adored the floral slaughter,

To know is to love is to pick
Is to love is to know,

He pushed a rose into the face
Of his girl saying, 'God is love,

That is why
He invents diseases'

(Or pounces in a railway
Carriage with a necktie

Taut between his fists
And a briefcase full of daffodils).

FORBIDDEN FOOD

1

In the dark we do not know our food
And this is the dark I mean.

It is the dark of Hadley Woods
Where cyclists in the garden
Of the Rising Sun ate strawberry jam
On bread, and loved the abundance
Of real fruit, until in the sudden blaze
Of fairy-lights, they found that the luscious
Lumps were not strawberries but wasps.

From then on they ate only
Illuminated food.

2

It is the dark of that first canteen
Where I ate with my eyes shut
The only food on the menu,
The food which flowed without end.

3

Each people fears it will fall
Into a soup of self-consumption,
And the malcontents, the friendless
Anti-social dupe us into this;
Develop our taste, with the greatest
Fear that halfway through
Our devilled pork chops we come
To our senses and see human
Hands there in the mustard.

By then it is too late.
All that is left of civilization

Is a rising pile of napkins
And dwindling queues at the checkouts.

Each fruit, each flower,
Each vegetable is contaminated
From marrow to mandrake;
Men fill our vases
And our plates, that's
Why those huge daisies
Smell of sick, why the beetroot
Leaves indelible stains.

Gardeners and gravediggers
Rub shoulders professionally,
But a blurring of the boundaries
Will mean the end of society.

4
There are salads beyond belief,
There are unimaginable sandwiches.

'The body of God the
Body of God the body
Of God the body of
God the body of God' Fish
Whimpered over and over
Tearfully as he tucked in,
His table manners questionable,
His knife and fork shaking,
His legs crossing, uncrossing,
His cheeks bulging,
The food nearly coming out again . . .
He shorted out Sing Sing's chair.

Or Kroll, who saved on the shopping
By taking his steaks

From the thighs of girls.
Think of that scum
Forming in his pan.
Think of that kitchen.
If there would you dare
Lift that lid,
Or watch him lift the steaming spoon
To test the flavours?
And later, drinking it off,
Watch him count through pfennigs
To see what he can buy.

5

The public called for blood.
How could they feast on poor cabin-boy Parker?
And so the foundlings rose from the dead
In the Falmouth courts to hear this:

The cannibals are terrible,
Should have their teeth cut out
Should be force-fed greens
Should be shunned by their own
Should be kept from kissing
Should see their food's trash,
Flesh into flesh makes maladies,
A *mal de mer* on a sea of blood,
Of men, man into man, *Homo sapiens*,
The very species might drown . . .

Something has just surfaced in the gene pool
And is climbing out and drying itself.

6

When the dead will come
To the dinner table,
but not to weep or scrape

At the cloth; they will
Sit in their stoneware thrones,
Their brittle chairs

Soaked in Bull's Blood
And juniper berries, in
Coats of aniseed and vinaigrette,

Jewellery of sweetcorn, scrubbed down
with all possible spices. We will
Hear them gossiping in ovens,

See their steams rise from the casserole
Like spring-morning breath.
A seasoned resurrection that

7
Strikes a match
In the dark dark dark
(This is the dark I meant),
The little eyes of captains,
Merchant bankers, eminent
Men of letters light up
And glisten in it,
The light from the match
That keeps on burning, not
That it has an infinite
Stalk, but because it burns
Wood it has already burned.

What brilliant food
Might we find in its light!

8
Can you stomach this?
There is a meal somewhere

That will never end,
Which needs no recipes
or ingredients and will
Fill our plate forever.

Can you smell it?
It has the smell
Of every meal that was ever cooked.
Eating it is like talking
With everyone that has ever lived.
Let us find it.

II HOUSEHOLDER

THE UNMADE BED

The unmade bed will stay
Unmade, proof of a night

Of healthy disturbances.
We could not have made

This mess unless we loved.
Only the houses of the dead

Are neat, and lunatics wake
To perfect sheets and ordered pillows.

Ours is a bed of tough
Vivid weeds in which the springs

Have come up like worms
From the dark underworld of shoes.

The pillows have lovebitten us.
We have slept folded in a soft weapon

Packed with triggers ready to shoot us,
Two human bullets, through the ceiling.

Sleeping is a risk, a fight, a chance.
Most of us will die in bed,

That is a fact, that is why
Walking across one can feel like treading

The shaky ground
That has dried over quicksand.

The unmade bed must stay unmade
For the day, until we're tired again;

Then we will stretch a sheet
Between us. It will tremble like a sail

Catching breath. We'll fold strong corners,
Knowing how much it takes to hold us.

LOFT WATER

I was frightened
Of the loft's lightness.
To stop it floating off

I wanted it tethered there,
Filled with a ballast
Of history, aerials, water.

Perhaps it was foolish
To drink from its tank
And risk the weight

Of the whole thing decreasing,
But on hot nights
I could not help

Swallowing until it hurt,
Water as cold
As if from earth.

And I sank into bed
Bloated as a fish,
Heavy with liquid, but still

A dangerously light anchor
For that kite of slate
I flew in sleep.

SINK SONG

Newtown after rain,
   Contrived upon odd
      Notions of balance –

The fulcrum of forks,
   Saucepans' centres of gravity –
      This city teeters

As its towers of offices
   And concrete theatres
      Recover from downpour.

My skin toughens
   At the sight of the grater,
      It must be cleaned backwards

To save my nails.
   Nor must I trap myself
      In the egg whisk's gears

Or stare too long
   At the sieve, its fencer's
      Face is threatening.

I must, however, dare
   Place my hand
      In the almost empty water

Knowing only knives are left,
   Like a child's hand
      Into a rockpool of crabs.

Their blades form final
   Stiff bouquets, but I have lost
      All my vases.

I mourn my crumpled
   Fingerprints. My nails, however,
      Are never so white as now.

THE COMING OF GAS

By the fire; the cat,
Myself and the mantelpiece.
The temple of flames.

I am watching the TV's
Blank screen and seeing
Windows in it,

The windows that are behind me
Where the curtains have thinned
To reveal the tall, white day.

Smoke is the monkey
That climbs the chimney's
Hollow tree.

The cat's patterned skin
Flattens, the envy
Of every tattooed man.

She expands like metal,
A moth-like alertness
To light and heat.

In my dream
White water
Poured from her head.

Her grey friend down the road
Is called Mr Smoke.
He climbs trees.

The white mantelpiece
With its two empty shelves
And classical columns,

Its last legs.
I was frightened when the blue men
Tore it from the wall

To show that only
A few black nails
Ever held it there.

I had thought it was part of the house.
These men, they introduced
New pipes to the house,

Bent them with their knees
To fit the corners of the wainscot,
Laughed rudely at the state

Of the old coals they hid forever
Behind their beige chipboard.
Now I close the curtains

And fill the television's
Olive green with pictures
That even the cat watches.

The mantelpiece?
Its white wood made
Our huge November bonfire.

GAS FIRE

Out of the miner's dark
The sea exhales
Into our living room.

I make his breath visible
With matches. Their dead
Selves assemble like runes.

Through dozens of windows
I see a view
Of orchards of oranges.

I am taught the spectrum.
I notice my finger hair
Has become brown ash.

Our eyes are tearless.
We can no more cry
Than an ant

For we are as dry
As insects,
Our skins brittle

And capable of ignition.
Our matches are half black,
There are thousands of them.

THE KETTLE'S STORY

The kettle can't keep his secret,
His hat is brimming with ideas,
He can't keep them in.
He decorates the air
With long curlicues
Of visible music,
Singing his history!
What is it the kettle has to tell me?

It begins when his cold waters
Consolidate in the Mendip cave
Of his furred insides.
He see-saws on the stove's cross
As his waters rock.
The sharp spikes of gas
Like a nest of precious eggs
Seem to fill him with joy.
Flakes of limescale shift
Like shells shunted by his
Closed ocean. Crowds of pearls
Form in his oyster darkness,
His riches accumulate,
His glass heart produces jewels
As it pounds, his body trembles
As though driven by engines,
I have excited him until
He has to shout like an evangelist
Of the stove, his long,
Broad, twisting shout
That plumes to the ceiling,
'I will have everything!'
He screams in his steam dominion;
In his power I am unable to touch him
Until I seal off his source of inspiration
And handle him carefully with a dishcloth.

I sip my tea and sit
Looking at the kettle.
He has told his story
But I will hear it again
And again try to understand it.
Meanwhile he sighs and waits
And bears his lukewarm waters like a burden.

WASH

This water saves us
Having to talk

As we wash upright
Like cattle,

Each other's young.
We run with wet

Like kitchen windows,
Upstairs among cumuli

Of talcum and steam,
Erasing ourselves

With towels.
Outside the black drains

Thrive on the wall
Like a vine.

HOUSEHOLDER

I can tell rooms
By their door-noises,
Which hinge is which.

I learnt the positions
Of light switches early,
Finding them like rare

Useless fruit
At the rooms' edges.
I smell the perfumes

Of the light bulbs.
I know when I am
Right under them.

The bannister guides me
Like a good child's hand
Through traffic.

The cold hall's
Tiles click against
My outdoor shoes.

I feel my way about
The landing on all fours,
Testing the carpet for holes.

Only the bathroom
Answers back. Its painkillers
Sound like teeth.

The house has explained
Itself to me, handle
By cold handle.

I shake hands
With doors. They
Close like overcoats.

LLANDDWYWE

I have built this farm
Many times now.
I heave its vast boulders

While my knife whittles through my meals
Like a ploughshare. With my fork
I stack peas and build

Its mountains out of mashed potato.
Its walls are a puzzle
That has solved itself.

I make gates of red iron
That squeak. I build
The cowshed bigger

Than the fat chapel itself
And fill it with the smell of women.
My cows are covered in pictures,

I feed them on yeast
And squeeze them of their weight,
They never moo during this.

Their terrace of cottage doors
Slams shut on windy nights
Like a train.

My daughter dresses like a man
In my old clothes.
Myself I have white hair

Spread like pages
From under my crumpled cap.
I lock my dogs in a windowless school

Where they yelp through their black lessons.
My tiny brass stand pipes
Are vicious with their water.

We are surrounded
By famous waterfalls.
My rooster's fold of bone

Opens when the storms form,
His wrinkled eyes light up.
The sky has the only electricity,

My farm is about darkness.
After dinner I bang
The enamel plate with a fork

To set the one bell dancing
On its wire
In the chapel's cote.

My bellman's arms ache
After hours of Sundays.
My farm is terribly heavy,

Built out of a mountain's left-overs.
My barn is an Egyptian tomb
Packed with gold

And one huge staircase of hay
That it would take hours to climb
Up to my dark, soft loft.

CARD HOUSE

Breathing terrifies us.
Fidgety weather threatens
At the windows. We can't trust

Our own fog.
We shut up.
Our hearts dance.

Card house, what
Keeps you up?
Not the trains

Nosing their way through
The suburbs, sniffing the ends
Of the gardens,

Their shocks rattling
Like a hundred milkmen. Not
The lovemakers upstairs

Going like carpenters conjoining
Clumsy dovetails,
Rocking the barometers.

Will you hold?
It seems bees have studied
Trigonometry in the living room.

I would beg each and every
Atom be still while I
Construct your final storey.

Two and three of clubs
Make their little roof while
Royalty creeps in the basement.

Complete, I test my engineering,
Let rain in at the windows,
Encourage heavily laden

Goods trains to crash,
Fuck the light fixtures
Out of their holes.

The world collapses now,
I see, while only you are firm
No matter how hard we breathe.

NAKEDNESS

At night I surrender
My daywear to the wardrobe.

The chair by the bed
Grows fat with jackets.

Under the stair I can count
Through a decade of coats.

The loft's darkness is made
Of the trousers of ancestors.

I sit naked on the bed
Between two strata of clothes

And another one forming here.
Is there nothing more to unbutton?

WOMAN COMING IN FROM THE RAIN

She enters with the slow elegance
Of a bishop and hangs her umbrella
On the hook of the hatstand.

Her coat opens like the doors of a church
And releases the flock of smells
That rain has made of her.

And when she enters the kitchen
She is soaked again by dinner-steam
And loves it,

Holds her face over the potato pan
And wears the balaclava of steam
That this gives her.

And her eyelids are full of steam tears
That make her eyes feel huge
As she watches her face through a gap

In the condensation of the mirror.
And she peels off the nerveless skin
Of her gloves

So that she may feel again,
And enjoys the wet textures
Of her cat's fur.

And as her body lives with flavours,
What dry sheaves of harvest wheat
Her husband's kiss feels to her.

FOR THE BIRDS

Next door feed birds on bread
Throwing it high so it falls in our yard
Like hail. All I see of them
Are hands, fingers spread, testing for rain.

As sparrows and tits dine on crumbs
Second volleys fall on them, littering
Their shoulders and backs, so that in flight
They shake off their bread like tablecloths.

Next door's breakfasts are behind lock and key.
At dawn I put my ear to the wall
And hear the tap of metal on shell,
The repeated rasp of toast . . .

They blot up yolk with strips of bread,
Scoop out the white like Chinese sculptors,
Tear stiff crusts with firm dentures,
Smash their empty egg shells to powder.

It is a frightening thing to hear through our wallpaper,
These alarmingly early breakfasts
Conducted in secrecy by an old couple
Unmarried and childless in a rented house.

Afterwards he will go out slowly
And button his collar, tieless like a priest
And scatters his bread, celebrating the many
Marriages that have happened in his back yard.

His dicky heart flies with the brides,
The newly-wed sparrows thankful
For the confetti that falls on them each day,
They build new shells out of it, the future bread-eaters.

At night old Mr Something's pipe
Pecks at his ash tray. I hear it.
I hear the soft blows of his wife
As she exercises their fat, white pillows.

WORK

The garden was the first earth,
And outside the first earth was turned.

The first garden was just there,
The next one had to be made.

She digs the black ground,
He hangs out white washing.

Wet shirts will water flowers,
Ripe flowers will scent shirts.

Wasps lick the last detergents,
Birds feed behind their backs

On woken worms, up too early.
Blackbirds fly through negligées

And wet their wings,
On soaps like wasps.

Garments dance.
Roses nod as excess rinse

Comes like rain from empty skies.
The first earth can rot. This is best.

III POWER STATION

TO A POWER STATION

I

You simmer your allotted districts,
Bringing a city's kettles to the boil,
Switched on with index fingers.

Your set of six vases, each of a size
To make me a tablecloth fly walking
In fear of elbows, are overgrown

With steam, like the flasks
Of film scientists who have discovered
The transformational brew.

II

You are strong under my stairs.
When the fuse blew
And we switched to candles

I played cats' cradle with you;
Threading your silver hair
I sewed you back together again.

(The wet raincoat dripped in the hall.)
I flicked the switch by the door
And watched you walk the bulb's tightrope.

III

The pylons crackle like sellotape unwinding.
The power station is tearing its hair out,
Threatening to overheat, turn its bricks red

And scatter them, like a child
Tired of its old toys
And wanting attention.

Then we are thankful for the cooling towers
As the power station takes a long
Draught from each and wipes its brow.

IV
Steam is the ghost of water
And rain the ghost of steam
As a flower is the ghost of a seed,

Honey the ghost of flowers
And bees the ghosts of honey.
This then is a ghost house.

I would boil myself if I had a big enough pan,
A Diogenes of the stove, knees to chin, turning
The rings full on, I would happily evaporate.

V
There is a village under wraps,
The church cloaked with oilcloth,
Windows newspapered, only the gardens vulnerable.

Cooling towers, your death is a television event.
I watched it on a day when strong winds
Filled the streets with reading matter.

Christmas arrived early in the village.
The cooling towers fell like gloves,
The thick weather made sills and flowers fat with dust.

SCIENCE

We were Greeks
Getting the world down
To fundamentals

Which were the foodstuffs
And other substances
Of the kitchen, our lab.

Built dams of bicarb
For vinegar to flood;
The resulting froth

Seemed a living thing.
Examined the way
Different things burn;

Salt, sauce, tea-leaves.
Found flames could be green
Like leeks.

We could have made anything
From these bases;
Cocoa, Omo, Lea & Perrin's,

A touch of the gas ring
And such things will live,
A race of kitchen emphemera.

Liquid, solid, gas,
All the ingredients
Scientists need.

Felt really Promethean
When we saw stale milk
Struggling out of its bottle.

THE NEW WORLD

At breakfast we design
Cities for children.
See, their cars

Move at their fingertips
Along malls of closed shops.
They have their hazards,

Forks lie like traps
Waiting to be sprung
And pierce their victims

With four small holes.
They avoid rock falls
Of breadcrumbs.

Their cars have no
Real doors.
Their fingers are engines.

And this central monument,
The statue of milk
That always has dew,

From here avenues
Of packets radiate
Like Washington.

Plates are roundabouts
Of murder. They steer
Past stains of pigment

Like artists' palettes
And halt at father's
Cliff of newspaper,

Colonised by words.
Breakfasts have their dangers.
At the table edge

The cloth falls like water
And we could tumble over together,
Columbus, in our small car!

THE ANTHROPOLOGY OF CAKES

The oven solves many problems,
Possesses ideas of order
Which it expresses upon cake mixture.

This is not cremation, it is
Constructive heat. The soots
Of the dead do not float from here,

Rather, inert matter is encouraged
To become cake. Beyond their
Doughy adolescence the cakes

Become beautiful, like buildings
Whose domes rise according
To some unseen plans.

So architecture and cake making
Are sibling sciences. Think
Of those towns we see as cake:

Bath, Eccles, Pontefract, Chelsea.
Their pastries and currants
Are populations in themselves.

THE CAKES OF RADCLIFFE

They are pale
In the shape of apples,
Lemons and pears.

Their sponge tears easily.
They have peel of icing
And leaves of hard sugar.

The paper miller,
Dazed by a dayful
Of whiteness passing him,

Purchases cakes for his family
Every evening at five o'clock.
His wife jokes about her weight.

His daughter always gasps
When handed an apple
As light as an egg shell.

The man who sells
Forties and Fifties
Motorbikes buys cakes

For his family as well.
His oiled hands stand out
Against the white coats of the cake women.

His father spent his life with machines
And now he loves handles,
Doors, hooks and old coins.

His children,
Vincent and Ariel,
Wait by the garden gate

And smile as they take
A white paper bag
From his black hands.

A HISTORY OF HAIR

The barber treats me like his own secret,
Giggles with his back-to-front-face
As he tells how hairdressing and history
Are both to be seen in the trichologist's mirror.
How a hatred of the pompadour
Prompted Rousseau's natural man
And the razor blade beat the hammer
As the world's first invention. Civilization,
He says, must strive beyond the mere
Barefaced until such time as barbers
Are unnecessary: a time of bald supermen.

As he says this my hair crashes silently
To the floor where it is swept up by a child
With a broom twice his height. Beyond him
Men await domestication, hair coming
From nearly every hole in their heads (the barber
Trims eyebrows and aural cavities at no
Extra charge). They read tabloids and weeklies,
Squinting at the print. They are hanging on
To humanity by their thin whiskers. The barber
Will see that they land safely in his chair.

The history of my hair is one of struggle.
It has changed colour of its own accord
Several times, has changed shape and texture.
It is a country unknown to me, above,
Like a notion of heaven, out of sight, something
I can never see but which is seen by everyone
I meet. I only have haircuts for others
And am resentful of the barber for this.
So are these men, comfortably overgrown, like
Gardens relaxing in the absence of the gardener.

Barberism is a dying trade. Three of his four
Chairs are always empty, their sinks dry,
Sterilizing cabinets uninhabited. I am a child
To this untidy war generation who still think
Brylcreem important. The last barber will die
Sooner than they think. The last pile of hair
Will be swept up by the barber's child.
The last locks will turn grey and long.
The final chapter of history will have a beard.

THE INVISIBLE PET SHOP

It is not the pets,
It is the fleas
Among the pets.

It is not the kittens,
It is the playful parasites
That gather in their little gut.

It is not the songbirds,
It is the reinforced
Woodlice congregating

At their trough
Of wayward rain.
It is not the colourful fish,

It is the worms whose lips
Bleed on the underside
Of the floor.

It is not the immaculate
Rats, it is the flukes
Who one day send ants

Mad so they climb
Exalted to the
Utmost of grass.

It is not the perfect
Terrapins, it is the aphids
Who gulp up bodyfuls.

It is not the pups,
It is the fleas
Who drink the pups.

HORSE

(For Penelope and Suzanne)

The horse has made alarm clocks
   Obsolete, waking us
     With bone instead of bells.

He has borrowed his neck
   From the snake, look,
     The way it bends.

Horses are made in golden-floored
   Shadowy factories by female
     Lapidarists who polish

All night their horses
   Into shape. Legs
     Are carved

Like Queen Anne tables, living
   Furniture of the fields,
     They are. Reading

Palms with their lips,
   Ripping grass up
     For their relentless dinners.

Given half a chance the sprightly
   Horse will become a snake.
     Watch this: My wife's

Tiny herd, asleep, walking
   Over her, grazing the little
     Hairs of her agricultural

Curves. And watch this:
   Horse playing. How he loves
     Saying yes.

BLACK COW

When will it end,
When grass ends?

Or will it go on,
This dinner, when grass

Is extinguished, to shrubs,
Trees, walls, towns,

And will the world itself
Be gnawed down to the core?

The cows don't care, chewing.
They are so casual

As they pull
The rugs from under us,

Their fist-thick
Tongues poke cud

Out of their cheeks.
We are eaten out

Of house and home.
I see it, the future,

Picked out of the square
Teeth of ruminants.

Who's to say their food's
Not worth a stripped world for?

Besides, it passes through the cows
And out again, good as new,

The world, and yet this eating
Disturbs me, it shouldn't, but does,

As if it held more weight
Than lazy glances credit.

This black cow's so black
No light comes off it. Young

Shoots pause on what
Lip there might be there

Before vanishing into one
Of four rumoured stomachs.

This solitary meal's how some
Say the universe will end;

All grass is falling
Down the hole of holes.

INDUSTRIAL INJURY

The metalwork lessons were of use
After all, he thought, as he sat

At his lathe in the Metal Box,
The machinery's symphony enough

To drive the mildest of men
To the edge of his seat. He thanked

Mr McCumsky as the clock bit
His card and allowed him to go.

That teacher's broken teeth taught him
All he needed to know

In the field of metal. His drills could scalp
Like Red Indians.

In his workshop a feebly drawn
Advert admonishing messing with drills

Depicted a feathered Apache
Chasing a schoolboy paleface with his tomahawk.

This couldn't happen to you but this could!
A child in his artisan's apron wept

By the drill, his bald head red,
Sketched by a real victim of such

An educational accident.
At Sperries his mother saw her best friend's

Finger lying in a pool of finger-blood, not knowing
It was a digit at the time, finding

Out later her friend couldn't point,
All those months at the typing school

Now well and truly wasted. And when
The glamorous firewoman fell

From the turntable ladder through fifty
Feet of untroubled air she hit

The ground in the following order –
Feet, knees, hands, face.

She survived but her face didn't,
Nor her famous Monroe hair

And thoughts of Red Indians come
Whooping back to say that this is not

Just a catalogue of gore, an inventory
Of nastiness, but that the sadness

Of industrial injuries brings the Marxist
Arguments right out, no matter how cosy

And classless the canteens seem,
Down below, chained to machines,

Mothers and fathers are losing their limbs,
Gently, casually, as if by someone

Feeding on grapes and he thinks
Of that latter-day blacksmith Mr McCumsky's

Bandaged glasses and his legendary
Way with a ferula, how children

Near him found their hands had turned
Into lobster claws and their eyes into

Broken eggs. He thinks of the cans he turns
On his lathe, thinks of the fingers he has

On each hand, kisses each one,
Counts to ten, if one day he reaches just nine

He will tear down the school
With what he has left,

He will run them down
Mr McCumsky's spine.

WORM

Dirt is myth.
This we learn
In our brown studies.

Dirt is house
Hearth and latch-key,
Mouth-shaped. Spat out.

Dirt is nakedness.
Where sunlight is vague.
Where rain is slow.

Dirt is roots.
Vegetation's beginnings,
Buildings' unpalatable foundations.

Dirt is history.
We hear all
Its footfalls.

GARLIC WALK

I

The sea smells of onions.
All its lines are parallel.

A tiny helicopter blows one wide ring
Which trembles on the water beneath it.

A thin pole of vapour, darkened by shadow,
Props up an enormous bank of cloud

That appears as flat as well-planed wood
And smoothly hinged at the tight horizon.

The evening is heavy-lidded
But even in this shadow

The thousands of white plants still shine.
I am told they are wild garlic

By a woman who fingers
The white lace of her blouse.

II

My young muscles trembled to ease up the lid
Of the baby grand. I thought the splint

That kept it up too thin to take
That great flat weight and thought

Of the butcheries that would take place
If it snapped and fell on my perched fingers.

The interior was its own auditorium,
The sounding board echoed like a door

To a mansion. And sometimes from the deep
Shadows beneath the portholes

And taut strings would come
An overwhelming smell of garlic

As though the piano were a garden
Of metal and bolted wood

That bloomed in the enormous night
Caused by the lid locked shut.

III
It was my brother who was gardener
To the piano as he kept time through his teeth,

Rich polonaises of his breath puffed
Through the web of the music rest

To infest the strings. The seat still warm,
I would attempt slow movements

But the sound was obscured by the stench
That rose as the strings trembled.

The machine perspired with human sweat.
My awkward fingers moved

More like a reader of braille
As my eyes strained at the dots of music.

IV
Was it the drink that made him play
The piano with his fists

Or the garlic, one raw clove of which
He would chew to fill a house with a smell

That he knew everyone hated? Did it make him
Pull a door off its hinge,

Tie a bell to his waist so that he would ring
As he walked the streets, clip the wires

Of the cat's whiskers, bite people's ankles
Like an upset dog, throw pans through windows

And enjoy the sound of the pane dismantling,
Argue with trains as they rumbled out of tunnels

In free fall, their castors keeping time
With the rails, was it the garlic

That made him show his wasted teeth, his
Spatulate finger-ends tear up his favourite books?

V
There is one particular path in Falmouth
That is so heavily laden with garlic

It is as if wardrobes of wedding dresses
Had been draped over the grass banks.

And even in the dark their smell still shines
And I cannot help taking one bell,

Crushing it and sniffing the smear
That remains on finger and thumb.

It is a hot-tempered smell. We walk terribly slowly
Along the path, breathed at from all sides,

Waves in the distance as slow
As the rhythms of our feet.

IV SUFFOLK INTERIOR

MEETING THE GREENGROCER

'Let the sky rain potatoes . . .'
                    – Falstaff

I was a thirsty baby.
I gulped all my mother's fluids up.
Even before I was born,
In my dolphin days,
I tugged at a loop of her
And drank her entire lake of brine.

She bought potatoes from the man
Who looked like Benjamin Britten.
He scooped the pink Lincolnshires up
From his tub in a silver dish
And weighed them.

Before I was born
He glared his red face
At my mother's middle.
I trembled with what few bones I had
In that rose-coloured light.

His shop was watched by fairground mirrors.
His fantasy was to eat young girls' breasts,
To have the blood running down his jaws.

I too was born with a red face.
I yawned, and the complexities of my mouth
Were demonstrated in their unfolding,
Such gusts and blustery showers there.
Weaned from her breasts I lived
On milk and potatoes
Each boiling side by side.
'Lift the covers of the boiling pans,' I sang,
'Sing the praises of the different steams!'

And munched on a bucketload of peelings.
The spuds became terribly delicate,
The milk boiled over and burned,
My mother was sick to see the black ashes.
I thought of the red-faced greengrocer
Weighing his face-coloured spuds
For more pale mothers.

GLOVES

I was more or less born
Wearing gloves, so I'm told –
My fists bound tight in bandages,
Two white boxing gloves
To protect my scabby nose.

The funny thing is
My mother died wearing gloves
Like socks on her hands.
In her madness she wanted
To scratch herself to pieces.

Funnier still my wife
Now wears gloves in bed –
Beautiful white lacy ones
Like bride's hands in sleep
To protect herself.

I imagine her making me in sleep
With her gloves,
Like a potter at her wheel.

THE DARK MORNINGS

They gave us armbands
Of fluorescent orange
For the dark mornings.

We were confused.
The clocks had lost their tightness,
The windows showed only us

As we washed in the kitchen
Where the stove sat like a judge,
His mind summing up

Four things at once.
The blank pans of water whispered,
'His name escapes me'.

The soap forced my hands in prayer
And gave me a face of alabaster.
On the dark mornings

We all hid our faces;
Behind soap,
Behind crackling newspapers,

Behind long hair combed forward
Sister's head on back-to-front;
It was all wrong.

It was no o'clock.
I only knew I had to wear
My bright armbands

Like waterwings
That kept me afloat
As I crawled to school

In currents of dark
Streets whose names
I forget.

GRANDFATHER'S ROCKING HORSE

Her father, the metal bender,
Comes home with hands scratched
As though he'd been playing with a cat.

He bathes her with his huge hands,
The fingernails white like front teeth,
Skin scored with hairlines of blood.

He grips her like his own huge vice
And stings her with boiling water.
She is for him to fold

As his ringing sheet metal
That creaks in its collapse
And dents his own paws.

In the corner Grandfather's rocking horse
Grins his Aztec grin
At her nakedness,

The enamel peeling from his teeth,
His mane like the frayed ends
Of a black rope of tar.

Beside him is her stringless violin.
But he has no hands,
Just wooden stumps fixed with bent nails.

Undressing her for bed,
Her mother wonders why
She never rides the rocking horse,

Then sees on her tiny,
Powdered white buttock
A bruise like a U.

THE BIG CATS

She sleeps in the boughs
Of the stairs' tall tree
And dreams of being eaten.

She has opened up
The dark continent
Of the house

With its forests
Thick as boot brushes.
She has even stepped

On the equator's straight thread,
(It passes right beneath her bed
Where two planes of lino meet).

Downstairs the savage carves
Circles out of carrot, onion,
Tugs at kitchen's cheap red meat,

While this girl
Whose dream it is
To feed herself to her cats

Sleeps on the great
Adventure of the staircase
With lion, jaguar, lynx;

A sort of Orpheus,
Her flesh is melody
To these beasts,

It makes them strong.
They lick their foot-soles clean.
They will last her a lifetime.

MANDRAX

I

In my dreams
The museum mouse
Came up the path,

The black glass
Fallen from his eyes,
Two tiny button holes.

I remember his friends;
The fox who had
A tongue of wax,

An owl, ghastly
In fixed flight,
His wings fingers of silk

And the kingfisher
Who lived in a cupboard,
His jaws dripping sap

As he fetched up
One tasteless fish
From his pool of glass.

They all shared
A forest entirely white,
Behind glass

And lit by neon;
Their feeble bodies
Packed with twine

Wound tight in knots,
Weak, unmuscular,
Their skulls quite empty

As was this mouse's head
As he crept into the house,
His eyes in his pink hands.

II
My mother's sleep was made
Of chalk. Round, white pills
That fixed her suddenly

In a peaceful paralysis.
Her egg, half hollowed-out,
Becoming dry and cold.

I imagined her
Inside the glass
Of her pill jar

Fixed in some transparent
Solution that was all
The sugars of the world

Crushed to one perfect
Mammoth ice
So sweet it burned.

Her book open
At every page.
Her glasses crooked.

She would go to bed
On all fours, her specs
Clatter on the carpet.

SUFFOLK INTERIOR

And when the brass vase she stole
From Stoke-by-Nayland
Was placed on the dresser

My brother restole it and sold it for scrap.
And when we lowered the venetian blinds
The kitchen was filled with belfry light.

And I remember the infinities of my train set
With the engine furiously figure-eighting
Whose motor smelt of struck flint.

And so my mother's theft made our house
A church, the bench ends of the chair backs
Felt like knee skin of a child that falls often.

And my father under the ellipse of the lampshade,
Haloed well in reading, knuckles
Digging into the folded wings of his cheek bones,

And the aftermath of the washing up
Where St Catherine's leper water
Cooled in the red basin,

And the darkness that stayed in the loft
That was roofed in slate slotted
Like feathers on a rook's back

And all the shadows were so old
That if you were to remove the walls
You would have a house of dark air still standing.

CHURCH MUSIC

In a county of plaster,
This church
Frescoed with nothing.

Deathwatch beetles
Swallow the roof
Through their polished lips,

Feasting on five hundred years
Of oak trees,
Nibbling their way to paradise.

And instruments
Illustrating silence;
The 'cello's varnished egg

Pregnant with sound,
And all the throats
Of the organ, breathless,

Its array of bath taps,
Vox humana, versatile
As a starling.

And the intestine
Of the French horn
Which, outstretched,

Would reach the roof,
Would deafen those shiny gluttons
In their long corridors

Fastened in their holy clothes
Like shoes.
Or the priest

Asleep in his carved vestry,
See him fall from the woodwork
Crushing his skull with his hands!

BULLNOSE

Its tread left
Cardiograms in sand.
We tapped the glass

Of the dashboard clocks
Like doctors, urging
Our father past ninety.

The needle once trembled
Beyond this to where
No more speeds exist.

Its horn was like an American train's.
We sounded it for fun
On empty roads.

The radiator was a hive
Of insects, their quick death
Glittering on coppery cells.

Water came from tear ducts
That wept as wipers
Cleared arcs of dirt.

The petrol cap sealed
A jar of scent,
The vivid fuel

That I would smear
On my mother's blue wrists
As she checked her face

In the secret mirror,
Pressing her lips together,
Red as brake lights . . .

SMOKER

What ascensions
My mother sits among,

All that drifting upwards
Of the smoke, with ash,

Counterpointed, falling.
I am not sure if the cigarette

Is not burning into her fingers
And she is going up

In that same way. For,
As all forensic experts know,

Humans, in their adoption of clothes,
Have made themselves

Into candles inside-out,
With wick on the outside

And wax within,
So that we burn slowly

And gently for hours and hours
Until even the hard old bones

Collapse to ash,
The rubble of us. And yet

Where the wax depletes
There is a foot, whole

And uncharred
With sock and shoe complete.

Beware the humble two-
Bar fire, it could be an agent

Of death by smouldering
If we were to slump unconscious

Across its filaments and burn
Like cigarettes themselves when left

Abandoned in the ash trays.
What smoke does the body give,

I wonder – black like tyre smoke,
Choking and bitter, or white

Like autumn bonfires, or perhaps
It is the blue of the overheating

Frying pan. What smell? Food,
I'd imagine, like a morning kitchen

Reeking of breakfasts, that same
Cooking smell, cooking sound

As kitchens go mad and take over.
Our chairs are for us

And us alone to sit in
As ash. Sing the praises

Of smoke. The smokers desire
This. My mother's lap

Is a lap of ash already
As she slowly burns away.

It shall become more
And more ash as

The days go by, the years,
Into ash and more ash.